Hell on Wheels

The Incredible Story of Rookie Roller Derby Queen Cindy McCoy

Karen Mueller Bryson

Hell on Wheels

Edited by Lea Ellen Borg (Night Owl Editing Services)

Published by Short on Time Books

www.shortontimebooks.com

This book represents the recollections, experiences and opinions of Cindy McCoy. All names, dates, incidents and sequences of events are as Cindy McCoy remembers them.

This book is dedicated to all of Cindy McCoy's fans.

Special thanks from Cindy –

Special thanks to Carol O'Conner of Australia. Without her one question, this book would never have been written. Carol is a very dear friend, who truly started everything.

Special thanks to my husband, Terrance O'Neill, who found the question and answered it. Terry has been instrumental in making this book come to life, with his strong will and determination to see this project completed. He has not taken no for an answer; thus we now have the book and our website and many new and dear friends as a result of all of his hard work and research.

Special thanks to Neil Donohoe for his friendship and all of the information furnished to us. His vast knowledge of the roller games in Australia was instrumental in the construction of the book and the website.

Special thanks to Murray Shoring for furnishing us with the names of people in the pictures taken at the photo op of The Silencers. This was such wonderful news. This information brought back so many wonderful memories.

Special thanks to John Hall, my mentor. He was my trainer, my manager, and my dear friend.

Special thanks to CBS News Channel 4 – Denver, Colorado for doing the interview with Gary Miller on the roller derby games.

Special thanks to the Denver Roller Dolls for making me an honorary member of the Roller Dolls.

Special, special thanks to my daughter, Tiffany, for all of her help and computer skills.

Special thanks to Clare Sanders for all of his hard work on our website.

Special thanks to Karen Bryson for writing my story.

Preface

The 1960s were the height of popularity for the roller derby, not just Down Under, but throughout the world. Australian fans were particularly enthralled with the sport and fans faithfully attended games every week. According to an article by Kerry Yates published in *The Australian Women's Weekly* (November 9, 1966), fans anxiously read about Roller Games gossip and many parents dressed their children in copies of the Los Angeles Thunderbirds' red, white and blue uniforms. The skaters became celebrities and were often mobbed by adoring fans. Many of the skaters received 200 or more fan letters per week. It was during this exciting era that skating legend, Cindy McCoy, became a superstar.

Cindy was just a teen when the honor of being named both Rookie of the Year and Queen of the Year was bestowed upon her. It is an honor that was never repeated, even nearly 50 years later. Cindy became a role model to young fans, and many girls even wore their hair just like Cindy, with her signature ribbon.

Cindy fondly remembers the fans being so excited, and they kept calling her their queen. At the time, Cindy didn't understand what they were talking about, but looking back, she believes it would have been such a warm wonderful moment, she could have shared with the fans, if she had the awareness of what had happened. It wasn't until 45 years later, that Cindy's husband, Terry O'Neill, discovered the story of Cindy's celebrity through emails with her former trainer, John Hall.

Terry found a question on the internet from an Australian fan, Carol, who asked: "Does anyone know what happened to Cindy McCoy"? Cindy and Terry emailed Carol, and have been in contact with her and several other people from Australia, who were fans when Cindy skated there. The fans brought back such wonderful memories; memories that Cindy now shares with her husband. Carol's one question put Cindy back in contact with John Hall, her mentor, her trainer, and her dear friend. That question also planted the seed for the creation of this biography of sports legend, Cindy McCoy.

Chapter One

Scott Stephens, who skated as "James Scott" with the Roller Games (an offshoot of the more famous Roller Derby) from 1978 through 1981, provides a wonderful history of roller derby and one of the sport's most popular teams, the Los Angeles Thunderbirds (www.latbirds.net).

According to Stephens, Herb Roberts, a former Roller Derby skater, founded the National Skating Derby, Inc. (NSD) and its first team, the Los Angeles Thunderbirds, in 1960. In 1961, the NSD was acquired by Bill Griffiths and Jerry Hill and the first games were played.

Within just a few years, the Los Angeles Thunderbirds become one of the most well-known teams in roller derby and their popularity matched that of other major league sports teams in the city. Throughout the 1960s and 1970s, the Thunderbirds' games were broadcast in Los Angeles and through-out the country. The Sunday night matches were amongst the highest rated television programs in the Los Angeles area. During the rapid growth era of the Roller Games in the 1960s, teams were established in cities throughout the United States and even spread to Canada, Mexico, Australia and Japan. The 1960s was the most successful period for the Roller Games and its popularity peaked in 1972.

It was around 1964 that the Roller Games were introduced to Australia, when American games were televised on Saturday afternoons and the viewing audience quickly grew. That's when Bill Griffiths, the executive director of the National Roller Games in the USA, decided to take some teams to tour Australia. The tours proved so successful that Griffiths decided to leave the Los Angeles Thunderbirds more permanently in Australia. It was at this time that Cindy McCoy traveled to Australia to join the Thunderbirds International team.

At just 5'6" with a slim figure, the attractive young woman, the "baby" of the roller team, looked more like a model than the typical participant of the roller derby. Cindy didn't have the tough appearance that many of her colleagues possessed, but little did her opponents know, she had a fighting spirit that would eventually make her a roller derby star.

The Roller Games had a great following in Australia. According an article by Kerry Yates (*The Australian Women's Weekly*, November 9, 1966) more than 20,000 fans viewed the Roller Games live each week and about a half a million viewers followed the games on television. At the time, the Roller Games were the biggest indoor spectator sport in the country.

Like teen idols, the skaters were often mobbed by fans and received hundreds of fan letters each week. But it was not without its controversy. With its banked tracks and high injury rate, many people claimed the sport was too rough for women.

Many skaters had a history of broken limbs and fractured ribs, but that didn't deter Cindy McCoy. The young rookie gave everything she had to the sport she loved. While other young women her age were shopping or worrying about her next date, Cindy was busy training to become a skating legend.

Chapter Two

Cindy McCoy was born in 1949 in Colorado Springs, Colorado. Her father, Archie C. McCoy, served in the army and with his wife, Maude Nellie McCoy, raised two kids. Cindy's older sister, Corrine Lee McCoy, who was born in 1947, had cerebral palsy, which Cindy says was the result of doctors using forceps during her delivery.

Cindy's family had a small two-bedroom home with one bathroom. Maude's mother, Rachel D. Simmons, lived with the family and she and Cindy shared a bedroom. The first word Cindy ever spoke was Babo, a name she called her grandmother until she was in high school when she began to refer to her as granny.

The family's home was in a quaint neighborhood with a beekeeper to the north and the local grocery just a few blocks away. Cindy and her mother would walk to the grocery on many occasions. Cindy spent a lot of her youthful days playing outside while her mother cared for her sister. Because Cindy had to think of ways to entertain herself, this sometimes led her into trouble.

One Saturday, Cindy decided to try imitating a Western program she had seen on television that had left quite an impression. She and her cousin, Darlia, were outside playing jump rope when the family cat, Murphy, crossed their path. Cindy decided to try and hang Murphy with the jump rope, just like the cowboys had hung the horse thief in the television Western. Hanging Murphy would be a test to see how it worked before the girls tried hanging each other.

Cindy and Darlia tied the jump rope around the porch pillar, tied the other end around Murphy's neck, and waited until the cat jumped off the railing. When Murphy started to make screeching, screaming sounds, Cindy's grandmother came running out to see what was going on, and went into hysterics. She grabbed Murphy and yelled to Cindy's mom to bring her some scissors. Granny saved Murphy's life. She also cut the jump rope up into a dozen pieces, and Cindy received the spanking of her life. It was many years before Cindy was allowed to have another jump rope.

Another incident Cindy recalls also demonstrates the fearlessness she would later need as a skater in the roller derby. It was a summer afternoon when she was just four or five. She decided to walk up to the grocery store, which was on the street where the city buses ran. There was an older couple waiting for the bus, and when the bus stopped to pick them up, Cindy hopped on the bus with them. This was at a time when there was no charge for kids to ride the bus. Cindy went to the back of the bus and sat down, so she could see all the sites and find out where the bus went. When the bus pulled into the bus station, the driver realized Cindy was the only one left on the bus. He asked her some questions and before she knew it, the police picked her up and gave her a ride home.

When the police asked Cindy why she was on the bus, she simply told them she just wanted to see where the bus went. When she arrived back home, with compliments of the Colorado Springs Police Department, Cindy's mother was hysterical. She had called Uncle Lee (granny's brother-in-law) to stay with Cindy's sister so that she could go looking for Cindy. She had no idea where Cindy had gone and was scared. Cindy says she felt badly and regretted causing her mother so much anguish. She promised her mom and the police that she would never get on the bus by herself again.

By the time Cindy was five, her family had moved to another part of town, where the kids had sidewalks to play hopscotch and skate with clamp-on skates. Their new neighborhood was right across from the grocery store.

Cindy started kindergarten in the fall of 1954. She was a little scared at first, but it only took her a short period of time before she fell in love with her teacher and enjoyed her classmates. She showed early signs of athleticism, with her love of physical activities such as the swings and monkey bars on the playground.

Cindy and her cousin, Darlia, continued to have adventures. Cindy's house had a big picture window in the front and birds would fly into it and kill themselves. Cindy and Darlia were upset by the birds injuries and the girls tried to save them. Sometimes they were successful, but other times they had to find boxes and dig holes in the back yard in order to give the birds a proper burial.

Like many kids of the time, Cindy and Darlia enjoyed playing cowboys and Indians in the backyard. They had a great time riding mother's broomstick for a horse. On one occasion, Cindy's dad had been doing some painting in the kitchen and dining room and had some leftover paint. Cindy and Darlia painted their faces with it because they were "on the war path." The girls both got their south ends spanked, and found out how harsh turpentine was when Cindy's mother and grandmother tried getting that paint off the girl's faces.

When Cindy was in first grade, her mother's brother, Uncle Gene, brought his ring-tailed monkey to Cindy's mom for her to keep, because his wife, Tammie, didn't want the "dirty thing" in her house. The monkey's name was Jingles, and Cindy thought he was entertaining. She would put him on a leash and take him outside for walks. On one walk, however, there was a problem. Cindy needed to get back home, but Jingles decided he wanted to go the opposite way. Cindy pulled on his leash, which made Jingles mad, and he bit her fingers. That was the last walk she took the monkey on.

When Darlia and Cindy had bananas or oranges for a snack, and Cindy's mom forgot to give

Jingles his snack, he would break out of his cage and come after the girls. If they didn't surrender their fruit snacks, the monkey would bite them on the fingers. After this went on for a while, Cindy's mom decided Jingles needed to go. She gave him to her sister, Dee. Jingles was happy living in the country and played with their dog until the day the dog got too rough and bit Jingles' hand. By the time Cindy's Aunt Dee found the monkey, he was too far gone and died.

When Cindy was seven, she had another "incident" with the police. She and her cousin, Darlia, were playing dress-up in her grandmother's bedroom and the girls got into some of the boxes where Granny kept nylon sheer curtains with big full ruffles. The girls decided to build a fort with the boxes and were hiding from Cindy's mom. When her mom called the cousins for lunch, they didn't answer.

Panicking, Cindy's mom phoned Uncle Lee to watch Cindy's sister, while she went to look for the girls. Cindy and Darlia thought it was funny and just kept quiet until they fell asleep in their hiding spot. When Cindy's mom was unable to find the girls, she phoned the police. While the officers were taking her mom's statement, Cindy and Darlia walked out of the bedroom into the front room. Needless to say, the two girls were punished and Cindy had to promise she would never do anything like that again.

Granny took Cindy and her mom to Elbert, Colorado to visit Aunt Dee and Uncle Lester about once a month. Cindy hated going out to the country because the ride seemed like it took forever, and she despised the rough and dusty roads. However, once they arrived at their home, a modest two-room log cabin with a porch, Cindy ended up having a good time playing with her cousins, Rita, Connie, and Jack.

The kids walked through the fields picking wild flowers and caught tadpoles down at the pond. They also played hopscotch in the dirt driveway, and enjoyed games of tag and hide and seek. Cindy's granny would always bring a cake or some delicious pastry she had made to share with everyone. Cindy remembers her granny being a great baker and cook. Cindy didn't realize at the time that she would later be forced to live with her aunt and uncle in their rustic home.

On her 8th birthday, Cindy was already show-ing signs of the independent spirit that would even-tually lead her to leave home as a teen to pursue a career as a professional skater. Cindy's mom gave Cindy her first birthday party and she was allowed to invite some of her friends and classmates to her home. When Cindy felt like the fun was over and the party was winding down, she decided to leave and walk over to the Safeway, which has a carnival and petting zoo set up in the vacant lot next door.

They featured pony rides and Cindy loved ponies; she hoped to catch a ride on one of them. Cindy was wearing a yellow dress with white lace that her grandmother had made her for her birthday. One of the ponies started chewing on Cindy's dress, and she didn't know quite what to do. Luckily, the operator came to her rescue.

But when Cindy's mom realized she was not at home, she knew where Cindy went, and came after her. She was so upset that Cindy would leave the house when she still had one guest at the party. Cindy was never allowed to have another birthday party.

But when Cindy's dad came home later that night after work, he had what would be Cindy's best present of all—a new sky blue bicycle with white fenders and a head light. Cindy has fond memories of her dad helping her until she was able to ride the bike without falling off.

Chapter Three

In 1959, Cindy entered the 5th grade, but she was already looking forward to graduating into 6th grade and being one of the big kids in school. Of course, junior high would not be too far off and it would be back to being one of the youngest in the school again. Cindy was between childhood and adolescence, a time when she could still play on the swings. She and her friends would tangle up their chains so they could spin very fast. Until one day, when a chain broke loose and Cindy got hit in the head. She ended up with a big black eye and scraps all along the side of her face. Of course, Cindy's mom was scared by the sight of the wounds, but she assured her mom she was just fine.

That summer, Cindy's mom and dad put Cindy's sister, Corrine, who was then 12, in the State Home and Training School. Cindy's dad struggled with the placement decision but Cindy's mom felt as though she had sacrificed her youth caring for her disabled child. Placing Corrine in the state home would provide Cindy's mom with some much desired relief, but her parent's decision completely broke Cindy's heart. She had an extremely difficult time understanding and accepting her sister's absence from the family. It was an act for which Cindy would never completely forgive her parents. Her carefree childhood days came to an abrupt end.

After the placement, Cindy's family was not allowed to visit Corrine for three months. It was during this time that Cindy's mom took Cindy to Skateland, where she learned to skate on the flat track. Cindy got to take lessons and skate at the rink on Saturdays. This began the foundation upon which Cindy would later build her professional skating career. Cindy also worked on jigsaw puzzles with her mom, and learned to play canasta. Although Cindy missed her sister, she enjoyed spending time with her mom.

Cindy says her mom was usually busy with taking care of their home and caring for her and her two cousins, Darlia and Rachell. Her mom had to prepare meals, do dishes, take care of the wash, clean the house and shop for groceries. Cindy says she often felt like she was in the way, so she found things to do to get out of her mom's hair and avoid disrupting her schedule. Cindy says after dinner, her dad often took care of the yard watering and mowing the grass and raking leaves. Cindy spent time with her dad, asking him questions. She considered it a very special bonding time with her father.

Cindy's dad worked for the Pepsi Bottling Company for a long time. After that, he maintained the road going up Pike's Peak. He also drove a water truck to take water to the top of Pike's Peak. The water truck was filled at a spring about halfway up the mountain and Cindy recalls there being a gift shop and snack bar at the mountain's peak.

Cindy has a number of positive memories of her father. When she was young, he spent a good deal of time with her. He taught her how to climb trees, catch worms for fishing, and ride the bike he bought her for her 8th birthday. She was so excited about and proud of the sky blue bike with white fenders on the front and back. It was even equipped with a basket, headlight and bell on the handlebars. Cindy's dad spent a lot of time with her until Cindy mastered her new ride and she was off to the races.

There was also the weekend Cindy went fishing with her dad and her dad's friend, Al. She was having fun learning how to cast until Al put bait on his hook and went to cast out. His hook caught Cindy's thumb and it hurt. Needless to say, Cindy was done with fishing because she didn't like getting hooked.

She recalls spending Thanksgivings in Kiowa, Colorado with her grandmother and grandfather McCoy, Uncle Mac and Aunt Elsie. They always spent Christmas back at home, though, because that's the way Cindy's father wanted things to be done. Cindy loved her father's extended family very much. She says they spoiled her in their own special ways. Cindy was always the center of attention and she loved every minute of it. She has fond memories of her grandfather holding her in his lap and rocking her in his big rocking chair. She also recalls her grandmother curling her hair in rag wraps, which resulted in long bouncy curls that looked great. Most of the time, however, Cindy wore her hair in a ponytail, so it was out of her face. This ponytail would later become one of Cindy's skating trademarks.

Cindy's Uncle Mac had a trailer house out in a back lot. She loved spending hours out there cleaning up for him or just simply enjoying the moments of peace and quiet. Uncle Mac ran the restaurant in town. He had been a baker in the navy and could really make a mean meal. Cindy enjoyed going there because her uncle always gave her one of his freshly baked homemade pies. The only thing that upset Cindy was that she was not allowed in the "back room" where the men played pool and card games.

Chapter Four

Unfortunately, when Cindy's dad started to drink, everything started to change for the family. It was the early 1960s, which was still a time of innocence in the United States. Kennedy was alive. So was Dr. Martin Luther King, Jr. America's young people had not yet started to protest the Vietnam War. Home life during the time was epitomized by the idyllic Cleaver family from *Leave it to Beaver*. Cindy's home life, however, was far from the perfect Cleavers.

Cindy's dad moved out of the house soon after their fishing trip. He had been drinking heavily and was doing strange things. Cindy recalls that her dad stopped coming home for dinner. Cindy's mom always had dinner ready for the family at 5:30 p.m., but when her dad's drinking got worse, he was no longer around for mealtime.

Cindy says one night when her dad finally did come home very late, she got out of bed because she heard him in the kitchen. She was excited to see her dad, but when she arrived in the kitchen, she found him standing in front of the kitchen sink urinating. In shock, Cindy said, "Dad, what are you doing?"

When her mom heard the noise, she also came into the kitchen and sent Cindy right to bed. Her parents got into an argument and Cindy's mom told her dad that he would need to start coming home for dinner. Cindy's mom said, "You can't keep going on like this. Just look at what you're doing to yourself and your family."

Cindy lost time with her dad because of his drinking. The alcoholism destroyed her family. Cindy thought she had in some way contributed to her dad's drinking and she wondered what she had done wrong. She felt ashamed and embarrassed, and didn't want anyone outside of the family to know what was happening.

Cindy's grandmother called her father a "no good S.O.B." and a "worthless drunken bastard." One night, she informed Cindy's dad that if he could stay out all night, them Cindy's mom could, too. Grandma, who loved to dance and usually went out on Friday and Saturday nights to a night club, told Cindy's mom to get dressed so they could go out. She took Cindy with her to the clubs and they had a great time, something Cindy's mom has not done in a long time.

After their outing, things in Cindy's house went from bad to worse. Cindy's dad packed his bags. She pleaded with her dad not to go and told him she would be good and not cause any problems. Cindy's begging didn't work, though. Cindy had previously begged her parents not to send her sister away; now she found herself begging for her father to stay. But all of her begging proved to be fruitless. Cindy lost her sister and her dad moved out anyway.

Once her dad left home, Cindy's life changed forever.

In order to support the family, Cindy's mom got her first job outside of the house. She started working at the 4-U Motel in housekeeping. It wasn't much, but at least it was a start.

Soon after, Cindy met her best friend, Sharon Marrs. She lived with her older sister and brother-in-law, after her parents had gotten a divorce. With Cindy's new home situation, Sharon became her supporter. The girls went everywhere together. Sharon filled a void for Cindy, something she needed at that point in her life. The girls road their bicycles all over the neighborhood for hours on end.

One day, they made a stop at a gas station at the top of the hill leading down to where Sharon lived. They needed to go the bathroom and couldn't wait until they got down to Sharon's house. Upon entering the bathroom, they saw a machine, which was broken and had boxes of Kotex in them. The girls were too young to know what the feminine hygiene products were used for, but decided that they would make a great tail to put on their bikes. The girls proceeded to tie the pads together and place them on the backs of their bikes. The two rode all over the neighborhood with the pad tails flapping in the breeze.

Eventually, the girls caught up with Cindy's mom on her way home from work. She was absolutely horrified when she saw the pad tails they had on their bikes, so she tore them off and gave the girls the third degree asking them where they'd gotten them. The girls told her what they had done, and Cindy's mom was so upset with the girls, she gave them a lecture on how bad they were, and told them taking things that didn't belong to them was wrong, and that they could go to jail for such things. Cindy didn't get to ride her bike for the next two weeks.

In 1960, Cindy began 6th grade. She was ashamed of the fact that her dad had moved out of the house. The other kids talked about it behind her back and made fun of her. Her home life made school difficult for Cindy. She became disruptive in class and got into fights with the kids making fun of her. The school administrators called Cindy's mom and asked to talk with her. They were confused, because Cindy had always been a good student. They decided that Cindy needed to go to counseling to help with her issues.

The counselor asked a lot of questions, and Cindy simply lied to her. She refused to tell the counselor what was really bothering her. When the counselor asked her simple questions, like how many brothers and sisters she had, Cindy would lie and say she had twelve brothers and sisters, even though she knew the counselor knew the truth. Cindy was putting the woman on notice that she was not going to answer her questions. Cindy felt her life was none of counselor's business.

At the end of the school year, Cindy learned that her best friend, Sharon, was going to move to Texas. Cindy couldn't bear the thought of losing her and wanted to go with her, but of course, she couldn't. Instead, Cindy exploded and picked a fight with Sharon because she hurt so badly. Sharon didn't have a clue what was wrong with Cindy and she never explained herself. Cindy said it was more than she could handle at the time. To this day, Cindy regrets picking the fight and destroying the friendship. It is something that still makes her sad to think about.

Cindy spent two weeks that summer living on the farm with her Aunt Dee and Uncle Lester in Elbert, Colorado. Her uncle had added on to the house, so there were more rooms, but Cindy's room was so small, it felt like she was sleeping in a sardine can. They also added running water inside the home, but they still used a wood burning stove for heat and cooking. They also had an outhouse that came with a duck that attacked and tried to pinch people as they came out of the latrine. Cindy thought her aunt and uncle's living situation was more like camping than a typical home.

When the two-week stay ended and her aunt and uncle took Cindy back to Colorado Springs, her granny told her aunt and uncle that Cindy's mom had taken off with some man. Her grandmother said, "She didn't leave a forwarding address and never even said goodbye." No one had any idea where Cindy's mom had gone or when she would be back.

Unfortunately, Cindy's grandmother could not take care of Cindy because she had to work and Cindy could not be left alone. Her grandmother said, "I can barely feed myself and now this house may have to go." So, Cindy's aunt and uncle took her back to Elbert to live with them while Cindy's grandmother scraped together some money to provide for Cindy's care.

Cindy was shocked, numb, hurt, scared, confused and embarrassed. She felt unloved and unwanted. She wondered what she had done to deserve being abandoned by both parents. She wondered if she had done something to cause her parents to leave her.

Cindy said, "All I could think of was, *Lord, what was going on? No one wanted me. No one loved me. Not even my own parents.*" Cindy said the hardship eventually caused her to learn to fight her own battles and to be a showman—skills that would come in handy on the skating track.

Chapter Five

By the time Cindy was in 7th grade, both of her parents were missing-in-action, and Cindy felt as though she was left behind. She was hurt and ashamed. She didn't know what she'd done wrong to have such bad things happen to her. She began to feel like a burden on her aunt and uncle. They were very poor and had very little, but they loved each other and their children. Cindy's aunt was a God-fearing woman and she always looked at the bright side of things rather than the down side.

Cindy's mom had grown up in Elbert, Colorado and her dad grew up in Kiowa, Colorado, which is a small farm community 10 miles north of Elbert. Everyone, in these farming communities, knew each other and their families. At this period in time, separations and divorces were not socially acceptable. Once people got married, they were expected to stay married. This put Cindy in a very uncomfortable position. She didn't want the other kids to know that she had been abandoned by her mother and father. Cindy said she did everything in her power to make sure no one found out the truth about her parents. She lied to hide the truth and told her classmates that she chose to go to school in Elbert.

The kids were mean to Cindy in many ways. She was ashamed of her aunt and uncle's home with no inside bathroom and no telephone. It was a hard pill for Cindy to swallow. Cindy said, "The situation was what it was and there was nothing I could do about it." She tried to hold her head up high and move forward. One of her teachers, Mr. Hood, told her to remember that beauty comes from within.

Things were not all bad for Cindy, however. Living on the farm, she learned to ride horses. Her Uncle Lester's dad had purchased two horses for his two younger sons, but the boys were not really interested in the horses. Cindy took the opportunity to ride, though, and her uncle's older brother, Dick, helped her to learn. Dick loved horses, and he shared that love of the animal with Cindy.

She spent hours riding through the fields in Elbert. When she rode, she felt free and at peace with everything. Riding gave her the strength to face another day. She found horseback riding to be a safe place. Lady, the horse Cindy rode most often, became her best friend. Cindy said she would ride for miles at a time and it gave her peace of mind. She could forget her troubles and enjoy the horse and the wide-open spaces. When she was riding, she no longer worried about the battles she had to fight and she didn't feel any pain.

Don, her uncle's youngest half-brother, went riding with Cindy on occasion. He was the more daring of the two younger sons. Cindy and Don rode for miles, raced the horses, and enjoyed the pleasure of being outside. One day, they were running late because they'd gone farther than they were supposed to go, and it was a mile around to the gate to get back to the house, so they decided to jump the cattle guard to save time.

Don went first because he was on Goldie, who was a quarter horse. The kids knew that if Goldie went first, then Cindy could get Lady, the little Paint she rode, over the guard. Don made it over, then Cindy put Lady to the test. The horse jumped the guard, but Cindy hit her foot on the post, and the barbed wire cut the top of her foot open. Although she knew she'd injured her foot, she didn't think too much about it for about a quarter of a mile.

That was until the cut started to hurt and blood began to run down her foot. The cut on the top of her foot was 2½ inches long and about ¼ inch deep. Cindy started crying because she was afraid to go back to the house. She was afraid they would never let her ride again. And she knew they would figure out she had gone much farther than they were allowed to go. The kids understood that they had no choice but to go back to the barn and take care of the horses, brush them down and give them some grain. They had worked very hard that day, and they had covered a lot of miles.

Cindy and Don both got into trouble and were not allowed to ride for a couple of weeks. Cindy's aunt dressed her wound the best she could, and Cindy had to keep her foot elevated for a couple of days due to the bleeding. The incident was one of several times Cindy was grounded for riding horses, rather than doing what she was supposed to do.

During her two and half years in Elbert, Cindy developed a hard protective shell and did not want anyone to enter into her space. She did not want to be hurt by anyone. She became a tough nut that no one could crack. Cindy wanted to make sure no one could ever hurt her again.

In 1962, when Cindy was 13 years old, her dad and his new girlfriend, Marge, showed up at Aunt Dee and Uncle Lester's doorstep. Cindy's dad introduced Marge to everyone and as time went on, her dad wanted to know if Cindy knew where her mom was and if she had completed their divorce papers. Cindy told him she had no idea what mom had done, and that she didn't have any information on her because she had gone to California with some guy. Cindy's dad informed her that he and his girlfriend were living in Goodland, Kansas, before the two headed off back to their home there.

Needless to say, her dad's visit had a great impact on Cindy. Seeing her father again brought back all of the hurt and pain Cindy had gone through when her dad first left. It took her three months to regain her composure and the experience added another layer to the hard shell exterior she'd developed. Cindy withdrew even more from people because she didn't want anyone to know she was an unwanted child. Being a child of divorce was hard enough at a time when divorce was not accepted; but being an abandoned child was unthinkable.

After school one day, Cindy had asked her Aunt Dee if she could spend the night with Barbara Hermes. There was some function going on at school, and she wanted to participate. Because they lived 5½ miles east of town, it wasn't always possible for Cindy to go back to the school due to lack of transportation. Aunt Dee told Cindy it would be okay, so she hiked about a quarter of a mile up to the big house where Mr. & Mrs. Bolejack lived to use the phone to call Barbara and let her know that she could spend the night with her. While she was there, Judy, Dick's first wife, had her horse out and saddled up, and she told Cindy she could ride her if she wanted to, so off Cindy went on Goldie.

When Cindy returned to her aunt's house covered in grass and with Duffy, a big coonhound, on her heels, something was clearly wrong. Cindy told her aunt that she couldn't remember what happened to her. The next thing she recalled was hearing the school bus stop and the kids getting on the bus. As Cindy sat up, her head started spinning and she was sick to her stomach.

Her aunt stayed up with her all night due to a severe concussion. Cindy could have fallen off of the horse, or she could have been bucked off. She doesn't remember what happened. Somehow, she ended up at Aunt Dee's, and Goldie ended up in the barn all lathered up. It took six weeks of rest before Cindy could ride the bus to school again.

Chapter Six

Cindy's transition from childhood to her teen years mirrored the transition the United States was going through in the 1960s. When Cindy was a child, life in the United States seemed much simpler. It was the period of "I Like Ike" and the Cold War. There were only three television stations and it seemed like America's only enemies were Communists.

As Cindy blossomed into her teen years, the Cuban missile crisis began to build and threatened the security of our nation's former bliss. Young men began getting drafted for the war in Vietnam and the USA elected its first Catholic President, John F. Kennedy, who was then assassinated. The Civil Rights Movement grew and the country began to march and protest. There was a revolution of music, culture, sexuality and drugs, and the country was divided by race, religion and war. Cindy came of age during this tumultuous period in American history.

Cindy had friends and classmates, who were drafted and served in Vietnam. Young men she knew came back home with missing limbs or eyes, head injuries, and mental illness from the experiences of war they had to endure. And those were the fortunate ones.

Others never came home at all. Cindy says she did not understand why we were in Vietnam and after learning more through research and study, feels it was a war we should have never been involved in. She says, "The events and things we were exposed to as young people have followed us through our lives. The young men, who served in Vietnam, are still wounded and will never be whole again. They have suffered a lifetime for our country. Yet, these men are now just statistics, and this means nothing to those in power, because they have not lived, or carried the heavy burden, as our troops have. These troops are our walking wounded until they die."

When Cindy was 13, in the summer of 1962, her mother and her mother's boyfriend, "Tex", appeared in Elbert, out of the blue, to visit Cindy. She was happy to see her mom, but Tex was another matter entirely. He was a flashy loudmouth, who thought a lot of himself. Since Cindy was so glad to see her mom, she overlooked Tex's attitude. Cindy's mom and Tex had been living in Whittier, California. By night, Tex played guitar in a small band, and by day, he was a painter.

Cindy's mom and Tex took Cindy to Denver for a weekend, and they went to Elitch Gardens, an amusement park, where they had a wonderful day riding rides and had lunch. Cindy's mom and Tex also introduced Cindy to some of their friends, Al and Neva Billings. The couple had three boys, all younger than Cindy, who were nice. They spent time with the Billings family at their home.

When Cindy's mom and Tex took her back to Elbert, school was about to begin. Cindy started high school in Elbert, which was not what she had envisioned, but she had little choice. On a positive note, Cindy was made prom queen for the fall festivities.

As her freshman year progressed, Cindy began experiencing severe pain in her hips and knees. She was in so much pain, she could barely walk. Cindy's Aunt Dee contacted Cindy's mom and she and Tex traveled back to Elbert. They took Cindy to a physician in Colorado Springs and he told Cindy's mom that Cindy had severe bursitis. As a result, Cindy would have to be on crutches for at least six to eight months. This presented a problem, because Cindy could not navigate the dirt path to the outhouse on crutches and the home in Elbert did not have an inside bathroom.

Cindy's mom and Tex talked with their friends, Al and Neva, and the Billings agreed to allow Cindy to stay at their house and attend Harrison High. The family had a means of transportation for Cindy and they were willing to take her into their home. Apparently, the couple had always wanted a girl.

Going back to school in Colorado Springs proved quite a change for Cindy. In Elbert, Cindy's school was very small and all the students knew each other. Cindy was in a class of seven students, three boys and four girls. Grades 1–12 were all under one roof with the younger kids at one of the building and the older kids at the opposite end of the building. The junior high students were in the center of the school. Cindy said the school had excellent teachers, who made sure they understood their studies.

In Colorado Springs, she was part of a class of 30 students, all of whom Cindy did not know. It was also the middle of the school year and she had to navigate the school corridors on crutches. She managed to do fairly well, in spite of her challenges, except in math class. Elbert was still using an old math system and Harrison High had changed to a new math system, which Cindy did not know. She also didn't get along with her math teacher, who she called, "a young arrogant ass."

After that school term, Cindy's mom and Tex, who had moved back to California, came back to Colorado to pick Cindy up and take her to California for the summer. They visited Knox Berry Farm, Disneyland, and the Roller Derby Games/Roller Games. This is when Cindy fell in love with the sport. From the moment of the first whistle, as the pivots and blockers took off, and on the second whistles, as the jammers sprinted forward, and as the two teams of skaters battled for their laps, Cindy was mesmerized. As she would later learn, jammers leave their team's pack and try to lap as many opposing players as possible. The other team members try to help the jammer break through while the opponents try to block him or her, often with a strike or hit. When Cindy saw the jammers score their points, she spontaneously jumped from her seat and began shouting at the top of her lungs. Cindy was hooked on the sport.

Tex bought a program for Cindy and she scrutinized it all night. The next morning, she was still examining the document. One advertisement especially caught her attention: New Skaters Wanted for Amateur Try-Out. That was a turning point for Cindy. She knew what she wanted to do with her life.

In 1963, Cindy was 14 and she ended up staying in California and starting school there. School in California was difficult for Cindy. The classes she was assigned were repeats from Colorado, where she had already covered the material. She says it was torture for her, but when she tried to get placed in different classes, they were all full. The placement in classes was purely based on the class that had room rather than student's interests or their level. There were so many students in the classes, Cindy says they were treated like numbers rather than people. Cindy was not impressed with the administration at all. She says, "They didn't seem to care if we were learning or not."

The school was also extremely spread out and the students had to move from building to building between classes. When the rainy season came, the students had to remove their shoes and run through water to go from class to class. Cindy also had some difficultly fitting in at school. Because she was a "country girl" rather than a "beachgoing California type," she simply did not fit in with the fast-paced cliques. There were also drugs in the school. Cindy says one girl who used drugs was found convulsing in the bathroom and almost died.

Because of Cindy's good looks, her mom wanted her to model for Catalina Swim Wear, and she even took her for an interview at a modeling agency, but Cindy never took a modeling job. Cindy says she did not feel comfortable with that type of work. She didn't like people objectifying her, and modeling did not represent who she was. She just could not come to grips with the type of work that would depend upon her good looks. It made her feel cheap and that was not who she was. She also didn't like the modeling business and didn't feel comfortable in that scene. It wasn't something she could see devoting her time and energy to. Skating, however, was another matter entirely. Cindy had become passionately devoted to the sport. She just needed to convince her mother of its value.

Cindy eventually showed her mom the ad in the Roller Derby Games program about their training school. Cindy's mom was hesitant at first, but she eventually relented when Cindy pleaded with her mom to let her check it.

Cindy had a pair of skates her mom had purchased for her from Skateland, but she figured out very quickly they wouldn't work on a banked track. She needed a 45-degree angle skate with no toe stops. Cindy ordered the skates and her mom signed a waiver for her to participate in the training school. She was off to the races.

At first, the coaches were hesitant to allow Cindy to train. She was young, petite and frail. She didn't look like many of the tougher girls who were part of the team, and they didn't want to see Cindy get hurt. But when they finally saw what Cindy was capable of—her fast footwork, skating speed and intense concentration—they were surprised and impressed.

The training wasn't easy for Cindy. She got banged up a lot and the remnants of the tough training, in the form of heavy bruises, occupied her body. Even as she experienced the pain of those training injuries for days after each intense session, her passion for the sport was never diminished. Cindy vowed never to go down for anyone.

Chapter Seven

Cindy trained and worked hard. John Hall, former Coach of the Detroit Devils, Head League Trainer for the Roller Games Training Center and General Manager of the Los Angeles Thunderbirds, was Cindy's primary trainer and mentor. Hall, who was ex-military, was awarded the Purple Heart. He was an imposing figure—6'3", black and 190 pounds of pure muscle. Cindy says Hall ran his training sessions like an Army Drill Sergeant and treated the skaters like they were in military boot camp. The harder the skaters worked, the harder Hall pushed them. If the skaters complained, or acted weak, Hall was in their face. Cindy says, "When you thought you couldn't go any longer, he put a foot up your butt and you went the extra 10 laps."

Cindy got so mad at Hall, her "Irish temper" flared, and she made up her mind that she would show him she had what it took to be a professional skater. She got tired of being told that she was "just a kid" and that she couldn't skate because she was too small. The more derogatory comments she heard, they more determined to succeed Cindy became. Skating became her obsession, her escape from a home life that she was ashamed of; skating was something she was proud of, and knew she could be a part of. Cindy's home life was not an issue on the banked track.

To be truly great in any field, one has to make a lot of sacrifices and Cindy was no exception. She made a number of sacrifices to become a truly great skater. One of those sacrifices was her schoolwork, as Cindy's studies sometimes took a back seat to her skating career. However, due to all of her hard work and dedication to the sport, Cindy quickly graduated to amateur status. As an amateur, she skated in games before the professionals skated in the Olympic Auditorium. The 9000-seat auditorium, which was built in 1924 for the 1932 Olympics, was the venue for a number of professional sporting events and was often used for roller derby games.

The pros from the different teams watched the amateurs skate to see if any of them might work on the pro teams. The recruiters looked for people who were fantastic skaters, had speed and were physically fit. In one game, a skater could expect to skate upwards of 20 miles, which required both training and athletic ability.

As Cindy worked with the amateur team, she learned the ropes. She contributed her heart and soul to the game and the amateur team started to win their games. Cindy also developed a winning attitude for the crowd. She learned how to play to the audience and charm them with her good looks and winning smile.

The marvelous highs of participating on a winning team came at a cost, however. Cindy also had some difficult times on the banked track. In one game, Cindy was a jammer, and Mary Holland, a heavy-set black woman, was the defense player on the other team. Mary and Cindy did not like each other from day one. The two were in competition with each other, fighting for a spot on a professional team. Because Cindy was so young, she didn't think she had it in her to be a professional skater.

In one particular jam, Cindy and Mary's skates got tangled up and Cindy's front wheels on her skate fell off. She fell forward and hit the inside edge of the track with the side of her face. The skin broke open over her left eye, and every time her pulse beat the blood would shoot out in a stream. When Cindy saw the blood, she passed out. She was carried up to the medical room, where the doctor cleaned up her wound and put two butterfly stitches over her eye. By this time, her eye was swollen shut, and black and blue. Cindy remembers the pro skaters gathering around to see the extent of her injury. To this day,

Cindy remembers Danny Riley saying, "Oh, she's just a baby. She's going to cry."

When Cindy heard that, she made up her mind not to let them ever see her cry. Although the cut stung like sin, and her head was pounding, Cindy simply told them she was okay. She said, "Please, just get me cleaned up so that I can move on." To everyone's surprise, Cindy mustered the strength to go back out on the track and finish the game.

When Cindy went home that evening, she didn't know what to tell her mom, because Cindy knew she would be very upset. Cindy went into the house and tried to keep her head turned away from her mom, so she wouldn't see her black eye. Of course, it didn't work. But Cindy reassured her mom that she was fine. She just had a headache, but she would survive.

After that game, Cindy received the call with an offer to skate on the international Los Angeles Thunderbirds team for three to four month. Her chance to be part of a professional team had finally arrived. There were a few spots open for the team's next season in Australia, and Cindy was invited to join them. They would be skating primarily in Sydney, Brisbane, and Melbourne on a weekly basis, but the home base would be in Sydney. If Cindy wanted the position, she would need to obtain a passport and be ready to leave within two weeks. Because she was underage, Cindy was also required to have her mother sign a release form and a document allowing her to travel with the team. Cindy was so excited.

Cindy was not adapting to the schools in California because there were so many students and all kinds of strange things going on. She never felt as though she quite fit in with the beach crowd. It was an extremely different environment than she had experienced in the schools in Colorado. Cindy promised her mom that if she let her skate for a while, she would finish school later. Skating was Cindy's priority, her way of surviving, and a means of escaping Tex, who had become a sick sexual predator. Skating was Cindy's fight for freedom.

Cindy's mom finally gave in, and Cindy was on her way to Australia within two weeks of the phone call. She was excited, scared of the unknown, and relieved all at the same time. It was difficult for Cindy to examine the emotions she was feeling at the time. She was on her way to a new adventure in her life, basically alone and on her own. At the age of 16, Cindy was a professional skater, traveling on the international team.

Chapter Eight

When the departure date arrived, Cindy was packed and ready to go. She traveled with a group of skaters that included: Toni Gandara, Judy Sowinski, Ralphie Valederaz, and Jo Jo Sanford. Cindy would join the Australian team, which had 13 members, six females and seven males. Nine of the skaters were Americans from the Los Angeles Thunderbirds and four of them were young Australian skaters. The hope was that the team would eventually be made up of an all-Australian team.

The group departed from LA International Airport for the 18-hour flight that included stops in Hawaii and Fiji before arriving in Sydney, Australia. Being the new kid on the block, Cindy didn't personally know any of her fellow skaters, but they would soon be a big part of the Los Angeles Thunderbirds International skating team in Australia.

As they were flying over the Pacific, Cindy noted that the Pacific Ocean looked so blue and so big below them. At one point, she could even see some fish in the water, which she thought was awesome. For Cindy, the first leg of the flight seemed like it took forever. When they stopped to change planes in Hawaii, they received beautiful leis upon landing. After a short layover, it was on to Fiji.

When they landed in Fiji, the plane doors were opened and the passengers were asked to stay in their seats. After additional crewmembers boarded the plane, they sprayed the inside of it with something that smelled so strong, it made the passengers cough and gag. Cindy was afraid of landing on the small island and her fears were not diminished when the passengers deplaned and were faced with indigenous Fijians in traditional costumes, with long spears in their hands and little clothing, standing all around the airport. Cindy didn't know whether it was all the television she had watched, but her imagination ran away with her, thinking about all the reasons those natives with spears might be at the airport. Cindy wasn't sure if she was safe or not, so she followed everyone else, ordered a juice to drink and waited until they could board the plane again.

Once they were back onboard, the plane headed for Sydney, and Cindy breathed a sigh of relief. Although they had a rough landing, their arrival in Australia meant they had lost a day, so they were all very tired and jet-lagged. Cars and taxis picked the skaters up at the airport and took them to three and four bedroom flats, where they would stay for a few weeks until arrangements for other accommodations were made. Cindy's flat had an old-style fridge, a gas-like fireplace for heat, and a milkman, who delivered milk in a horse drawn wagon. This was all new for Cindy, but the older skaters seemed to have a handle on everything.

Cindy had a number of things to learn from being immersed in a new culture. She had to learn about shilling and pounds, which was the local currency at the time. Australia is an independent nation within the British Commonwealth. In 1910, the country adopted a system of Australian pounds that was distinct from British pound sterling. The Australian pound was replaced with the Australian dollar, their current currency, in February 1966.

Cindy also had to learn Australian slang terms, because she had a lot of difficulty understanding what the Australians were talking about. Although the majority of Australians speak English, Australian English has a distinct vocabulary, pronunciation and accent, as well as their own slang words and regional variations. After some time, Cindy was able to catch on to the conversations with the Australian people.

Other customs, like playing the national anthem at the start of a movie, were anxiety producing at first. Cindy was scared when everyone in the audience suddenly stood up at the start of *Alfie* and she did not have a clue what was going on. Cindy stood like everyone else, but it took her a few moments to figure out they were playing the Australian national anthem.

Alan Rhyland, the trainer for the international team, had assembled a motley group of skaters, including Cindy, who would all vie for the coveted top slots on the team. On the track, only five men, or women, made up the competing team and the men and women's teams alternated every twelve minutes. The top players could also earn the most money. At the time, players would make from $100 to $400 dollars per week, plus bonuses for winning a game. Today, that salary would be about $700 to $2,800 per week.

Cindy quickly realized she would have toughen up and be both physically and emotionally strong if she expected to make the top tier, which was the starting team. Although she was young and had a small stature, some of her teammates came to view Cindy as a real threat.

The training was intense as the "wanna-be" players, young up-and-comers and has-beens, competed for top positions. Several skaters sustained injuries as they tried to prove they had the skill, speed and overall performance to qualify for the top positions. Cindy worked hard and was eventually one of the skaters selected for the starting lineup.

The skaters soon developed a routine. They skated in Sydney Stadium on Wednesday evening. Then, on Thursday morning, they flew to Brisbane to skate Thursday and Friday evenings there. They returned to Sydney where they skated on Saturday nights. Then they flew to Melbourne, where they skated on Sunday. Cindy says they had some wild plane rides due to bad weather and there were a few times when she thought they were done for when the small planes hit turbulence and the flights got very rough.

When the skaters returned to Sydney, they had Monday and Tuesdays free to do laundry, shop and take care of their personal needs. Sometimes the skaters went to movies, or shows.

On several occasions, the skaters were asked to do some public relations work. The skaters had a photo op on the film *The Silencers*, which starred Dean Martin as superspy Matt Helm. Cindy says the promotion of the film was a fun time. The skaters got to meet some of the radio and TV personalities of Brisbane. Players Ann Calvello, Carol Wilson, and Cindy were at this photo op, along with Don Secombe (former newsreader and host of a television show called *I've Got a Secret*), radio and sometimes television celebrity Bert Robertson, and Ron Cadee from *I've Got a Secret*. According to Cindy, the three gentlemen were awesome. They were funny and totally into the photo op. They treated skaters like royalty, and made it their mission to make sure they enjoyed themselves. On these shoots, Cindy never really got a heads-up on what the photo op was going to entail, so she was always totally in awe of everything going on. Cindy says she and the other skaters had a lot of laughs when they pointed their plastic guns at the film promoters. These three men made the skaters feel so comfortable, welcomed, and were totally into their jobs at this promotion.

The skaters were also invited to do a linoleum commercial with an elephant. They had to skate across the floor covering, and this is where the elephant came into play. The elephant walked on the linoleum flooring with them. Cindy says the skating was fun, but the elephant really made her nervous because it kept putting it's trunk around her waist. The handler was just a short little man, and Cindy was not convinced that he could control such a large elephant. The trainer had no difficulty with his animal, however, and thought it was funny that Cindy was fearful of the creature.

Cindy also remembers fondly a time the skaters went out in the bay with "the frogmen" trolling for sharks. The frogmen took the skaters out on their boat. They were throwing meat overboard to attract hammerhead sharks. They made fun of Cindy because she was afraid of the sharks, and didn't want to be anywhere near them. Cindy doesn't remember the purpose of the procedure; she just remembers she was afraid of sharks.

When the frogmen prepared a meal for the skaters, they gave Cindy a hard time, because they thought she wasted too much time eating. They said she didn't know how to use her fork efficiently, and told her not to exchange hands, but instead, to just simply cut a piece of meat and pile the potatoes and veggies on top and pop it into her mouth; and while chewing, then get another bite ready to go.

Cindy truly enjoyed her time with the frog-men. She thought the frog men were a great group, funny and entertaining. They really made the skaters feel welcomed and right at home with them.

Cindy and the other skaters also traveled in a hydroplane boat out across the bay, and went over to the Sydney Opera House. Cindy thought the sight was beautiful and breathtaking, impressive and massive.

A lot of promotional shots of the skaters were also taken while they enjoyed Brisbane. Cindy remembers one special holiday weekend the skaters had there. They spent a weekend holiday on the beaches with their beautiful sand and water. Unfortunately, they had to get out of the water on the second day because of sharks, and after that scare, Cindy did not go back into the water. She decided the water was their home, not hers, and she would stay out of the ocean. It was such a wonderful place, and the skaters had so much fun just being tourists, not performers or promoters, and enjoying the beautiful beach.

The skaters also visited the Lone Pine Koala Sanctuary, where Cindy got the opportunity to hold a real live koala bear, which was quite an exciting thing for her. Although the animal was extremely cute, Cindy was scared because she didn't know what the koala might do. Fortunately, she remained totally calm throughout the whole ordeal.

She also remembers an encounter with a pesky ostrich. While they were touring the park, the ostrich decided it liked Porky Parker and tried to hump him. It was a situation Parker didn't know how to handle, so they had to get a worker to take care of the unusual situation. Of course, Parker was teased relentlessly about his encounter with that horny bird!

Ann, Carol, and Cindy were interviewed and taken to breakfast by the reporter, Veritas. This was in Melbourne, and was truly a wonderful breakfast. They had about 16,000 fans who came to the games in Festival Hall. Following that event, Ralphie, Mannie, Ann and Cindy stayed over in Melbourne as guests of the famous Melbourne Football Club to join them on their visit to Sale, Victoria on the following Monday.

The Football Club put the skaters up in the Southern Cross Hotel as their guests. On Monday, they were transported by a cavalcade of cars to Sale, Victoria. This was the first and only time that Cindy rode in a Rolls Royce vehicle, which she thought was a beautiful, magnificent auto. The gentleman Cindy was riding with was so proud of his car, and he couldn't believe how impressed Cindy was with him and his vehicle.

This is something she would have never dreamed of, to travel in this type of style. They truly made Cindy feel so very special. Cindy doesn't have words to describe how impressed she was with all of the attention. It was like a fairy tale, a storybook trip. The Australian people opened up their arms to the skaters and treated all of them like royalty. Cindy was truly riding high on the clouds, and they gave her so much, and made her feel good about herself.

Chapter Nine

Eventually, the strict weekly skating schedule became very tiring for Cindy. When Thanksgiving and Christmas came and went, she became very homesick, and called her mother and told her she wanted to come home. Her mom contacted the administration office in Los Angeles, and they made arrangements for Cindy to go back to the United States. Cindy was happy to be going back to her homeland, although it was a bit unnerving to fly back alone. When she finally arrived, Cindy was glad to see her mom.

It didn't take very long, however, for Cindy to realize she had made a terrible mistake returning home. During the 1960s, there was a lot of unrest in the US. It was the time of the infamous Watts Riots, and Cindy says she did not understand much of what was going on in the Civil Rights Movement until much later. Because she was raised never to hate or hurt people, she did not understand the racism and hate involved. Cindy says she only learned what hate felt like when she traveled to Little Rock, Arkansas and it scared her. Cindy believes that civil rights have improved since the 1960s, but that people are still hated because of the color of their skin, which makes her sad. She says, "Hate is like a cancer. It is not going away."

On their way home from the airport, Cindy and her mom, had to go through Watts, and the people were scared. The looting had started and Cindy witnessed people carrying sofas down the street from the windows in businesses that had been broken out. When they were stopped at a red light, Cindy remembers an older black women standing out in her yard by her fence, and yelling, "You'd better get your white asses out of here before you get hurt!" She looked scared, and Cindy remembers feeling so sorry for her. Cindy had no clue what was going on, or why the people were in this type of situation. Never in her short life had Cindy ever seen anything like it. People were destroying property and stealing. They seemed scared, angry, and hostile. It was not a wonderful event to come home to.

The situation with her home life was even more difficult than when she left. Her mother's boyfriend, Tex, had become even more sexually aggressive and his advances were intensifying as each day passed. Cindy says Tex made a habit of saying things that made her feel uncomfortable. He would bump up against her and tell her she should wear her skirts shorter or low cut tops to "give guys something to look at" and "fit in just fine." He also told Cindy that he could "teach her what to do to be liked." Cindy says she had to keep her distance because he was so "handsy."

One time, Cindy caught him kissing and fondling a neighborhood girl that Cindy hung out with. Cindy went nuts and told Tex that she was going to tell her mother exactly what she saw. On her way to the nursing home where her mom worked, Cindy says Tex caught up to her and stopped her before she could enter the building. As they were arguing, Tex said, "And who have you been sleeping with anyway, you little bitch?"

Infuriated, Cindy lunged forward at him and kneed him in the groin. She then dug her fingernails into his face and said, "You're one ugly ass and now you're going to be even uglier!"

Cindy's mom ran out of the building and was finally able to convince Cindy to let go of Tex's face. Cindy's mom wanted to know what was going on and Tex lied to her face.

The fight had attracted a crowd and everyone watching assumed Cindy was in the wrong and were sympathizing with Tex. Cindy's mom wanted Cindy to apologize, but Cindy refused. She told her mom it would be a cold day in hell before she would ever do that. Then she turned to Tex and said, "If you ever come near me or my friend again, I will boil you in oil while you sleep. You think you hurt now? You come near me again and you'll find out what hurt is all about."

Cindy says she's not proud of what she did, but she felt it was the only way to handle a person as sick as Tex. Cindy isn't sure if there were child abuse laws in California then, but she believes today, Tex would have been put in jail for the things he did to children and would have been a registered sex offender. Cindy says she was ashamed of her mom living in a common law marriage with Tex and she didn't want anyone to know the truth. She says her mom made a big deal about her never telling anyone the truth or they would all be in trouble. Cindy believed her.

Cindy still feels uncomfortable about this part of her life, but she says she is revealing it, because it may help someone else who is in a similar situation. She says, "I want young people to understand it is all right to ask for help when they know that something happening to them or a friend is wrong."

Cindy also realized she would not be skating much in the States because the teams had all the skaters they needed! She was devastated at that prospect because she was a skater. She needed to skate.

Cindy talked with her mom and explained that she had made a terrible decision in returning back home. She told her mom she wanted to return to Australia to skate. She felt her place was on the international team and that is where she belonged. Cindy's mom gave in to her once again, so Cindy made a call to the LA office and told them that she wanted to go back to Australia to skate, if that was a possibility. She promised them that she would stay Down Under indefinitely, that she had made a mistake in returning to the States because she was homesick. She explained she was beyond that issue in her life. Cindy said, "My life is skating, and I truly miss the Australian people. They are strong and true, and I miss that strength in my life."

The Los Angeles office agreed to send Cindy back, and soon she was on a plane headed Down Under, back to Australia once again. By this time, flying wasn't a big deal for her anymore. She had gotten used to flying every week when she was in Australia. Flying had become a routine part of her life. Cindy remembers a couple of scary flights, though, when they were caught up in bad storms. The plane would drop two or three hundred feet at a time, and the lightning was unbelievable. She also remembers how scared the skaters all were on one flight. Ralphie Valladares, coach of the men's team, was only 5'2", but could out-skate anyone. He was a giant on the track, but became like a scared boy when flying. He was afraid of flying and he never got over his fear. He had white knuckles from holding onto the seat arm so tight, so the other skaters called him White Knuckles Ralphie.

Chapter Ten

Upon her return to Australia, and back to skating on the banked track, Cindy started imitating the captain of the woman's team, Ann Calvello, and her way of doing business. Cindy says Ann had a daughter and husband, who she left to pursue her skating career. Ann went to great lengths to stand out from the other skaters. She was always loud and stirring things up. Ann was well-known for her colorful character and multi-colored hair. When Ann first arrived in Australia, fans referred to her as "The Jolly Green Giant" because she wore her hair green. It didn't take her long to move on to more unique color combinations like pink and red spots, or red, white and blue stripes, and for the wild colors to become her trademark.

Cindy went to the beauty shop where Ann went to get her hair dyed a different color every week, and Cindy had a guy put her hair up into elaborate "big hair" curls. This went on for about a month. Cindy went to the night clubs that Ann frequented with her silver challis, from which she drank her vodka. Ann was quite an act to try and follow! Looking back, Cindy believes that it was because Ann was getting older that she had to resort to showmanship and antics to keep drawing appeal from the fans. Her body was aging, getting stiff and less mobile than the younger skaters, and she was having greater difficulty keeping up with them on the track. The antics kept Ann in the public's attention when her skating no longer could.

Other young Australian skaters started following suit with the imitation of Ann for a while. It all came to an end when Cindy was paid a visit from her original trainer, John Hall, who the main office sent to Australia to find out what was going on. They all wanted to know what the heck Cindy was doing. John promptly asked Cindy what the hell she thought she was doing and Cindy was hit in the face with the idea that she could never be someone she was not; she had to be herself.

Cindy says Hall made her realize that she couldn't imitate other skaters, even if they were her idols. She needed to use her knowledge and talent and be herself. Cindy says the "ass chewing" that Hall gave her was like none she had ever had in her life, but as a result, she evolved into a great skater and icon.

Soon after, Cindy's appearance went back to being who she was—a young girl with a ponytail, who had long hair and let it flow! From that point on, Cindy was the baby of the team, and she accepted that fact. There was not another skater on the team who could compete with that. Cindy was growing and getting stronger, and members of her growing fan base loved her for who she was, a young female skater, who they adopted and supported.

Some Australians predicted that the pulling power of the roller games would wane, but while Cindy was skating, the games were still drawing upwards of 20,000 fans per week, with a half million more following the sport on television. Being the baby of the team endeared her to those Australian fans and eventually made her a star.

Cindy was not extremely close with many of her teammates because she was so much younger. Most of them called her "the kid" rather than her name, and didn't pay much attention to her.

Cindy says Ralphie, a Mexican American, who held the world speed record for skating at 35 miles per hour, was very short and fast. Ralphie skated with the Thunderbirds for over 30 years, beginning in 1961 and ending his career in 1993. He held records for all-time scorer, most games skated, and most years skated. What Cindy remembers most about Ralphie, is that he liked to chase after women. He was in competition with the other men on the team to see who could "score" first. Ronnie Raines, who was originally a flat track speed skater and world record holder for the mile, was also a womanizer. Cindy describes him as a "hot dog", high strung and hot-tempered. Ronnie and Mannie Servin liked to chase the females. Mannie was Ronnnie's wingman. Cindy says JoJo Stafford, a tall skinny black man, was a talented skater with a lot of moves. Cindy considered JoJo to be her guardian angel and protector. He watched out for Cindy and made sure she was all right.

Two female skaters took Cindy under their wing. Toni Gandera, who Cindy said was the nicest of the American skaters, was a very easy going Mexican American, who played all the positions. Colleen Richardson, who was an Australian skater, was married and had two children. Colleen befriended Cindy and became somewhat of a travel mate. Both Toni and Colleen made Cindy feel comfortable and were kind to her. They sometimes teased Cindy because she did not know about or understand things, but they made Cindy grow as an individual.

Colleen and Toni took Cindy out shopping and to the salon to get their hair done. Cindy says both women were a joy to be around and the times she spent with them were very special to her.

Cindy says another female player, Carol "Flip" Philips, from the Virgin Islands, liked both men and women. She got pregnant while they were on tour and had to return home. After that, Carol swore off men and said she would stay with women because they couldn't get her pregnant again. Cindy says Carol was a comedian, always saying something off the wall, which would make Cindy laugh.

Cindy also shared some special times with a young man named Dennis, who was President of the Cindy McCoy Fan Club in Brisbane. He was slender, blond, very sweet and kind. She remembers that Dennis taught her how to drive his car, which was interesting, because in Australia, the steering wheel is on the right side of the car, rather than on the left, as it is in the USA. Dennis and a group of women would have Cindy and some of the other skaters to their homes for potlucks and they took the skaters on tours of Brisbane. They were gracious hosts and heart-warming, charming people.

Things were not all rosy on the track for Cindy, however. There was another young skater, who came up the ranks with Cindy in the United States. She and Cindy did not like each other. She was a defensive player and was older and bigger than Cindy. Because they were vying for positions on teams, the two became very competitive. Cindy's rival was black and Cindy says she would come at her aggressively and threaten her with, "I'm going to kick your white ass." Cindy retaliated by hitting her in the head with a skate. Fortunately, two other skaters held her rival back and told Cindy to get the hell out of there while they kept her under control.

When Cindy's rival was picked up by a team in Australia, they were skating against each other once again. Because Cindy was a jammer and her rival was a defensive player, they came into physical contact with each other. Cindy says that players resorted to many "dirty tricks" to take down opposing players, including rubbing resin from the track into their eyes, headlocking and ramming them into the railing or holding their shorts so they could run the skater into the railing or even throwing chairs onto the track. One trick that Cindy pulled on her rival was especially wicked.

When her rival went to the beauty shop to her hair done, they did something which caused her hair to fall out, so her rival had to start wearing a wig. Being young, and having an "I'll get even" mentality, Cindy did a mean-spirited thing by attacking her rival's wig and pulling it off during their games. Cindy would grab the wig, and while her rival covered her head, Cindy would score. Cindy continued to do this throughout the series against her rival's team. She realizes this was not a very nice thing to do, but she says it felt better than getting punched by the woman. Cindy was later told her rival didn't last too long in the sport because of her bad temper.

Cindy was also thrown out of a game for kicking a referee, Al Costa, in the groin. She says she didn't do it on purpose, though. Cindy was involved in a fight on the track and Al attempted to stop it. Cindy was afraid to let go of the other skater because she didn't want the woman to get the best of her. Al had Cindy by the legs, but he lost his grip on her and she clipped him in the balls. When the fight was finally broken up, Cindy was ejected from the game.

Cindy celebrated her 17th birthday Down Under. She continued to skate until October 1966, when she injured her back in a training session in Brisbane. Cindy was now helping to train other young skaters and she lost her temper when they would not fall correctly.

It was a Friday morning, and Cindy took a hard fall in the corner of the track and landed on the support beam, directly on her tailbone. The pain was unbearable and Cindy's legs went numb. It took every ounce of courage she could muster to get up, get off the track and into dressing room. It hurt to stand, it hurt to sit, and it simply hurt to move. Colleen Richardson was with her at the time, and Cindy told the young amateurs to take another five laps and call it a day. Colleen realized that Cindy was really hurt, and she came into the dressing room and aided Cindy. She took Cindy's skates off of her feet, helped her get dressed and called a cab so they could return to the hotel, where they were staying.

Upon their arrival, they entered the hotel room, where Cindy believes Tony Gandera and Judy Sowinski were, and Cindy told them that she thought she had really hurt herself. She collapsed face down onto the bed, and began to sob uncontrollably. Cindy couldn't stop herself. She was in so much pain and was truly scared. The other skaters tried to get Cindy to take a shower, but she couldn't stand the pain. She got sick to her stomach and started to sweat and cry. Tony and Judy contacted the office and made arrangements for Cindy to go the hospital. Cindy doesn't remember a lot of details because of the pain she experienced. She remembers receiving some initial medical care, and being given pain medication.

Cindy was not doing well. She had dislocated her tailbone and fractured the last vertebrae in her back. There was quite a bit of nerve damage and she lost a lot of the feeling in her legs. Cindy believes that she probably injured herself in the prior nights' games, but not enough to put her down, then the fall in the training session finished the job.

Cindy returned to Sydney and underwent surgery, during which the doctors realigned her tailbone back into position with a permanent pin. The doctors told Cindy that getting her to walk normally again would be a major achievement. She was told that she would have to be bedridden in the hospital for a while because she had done so much damage to the nerves in her lower back.

The doctors told Cindy if she did not follow their instructions, she might not regain the feeling in her legs, and that she probably would not skate, bowl, or ride horses ever again. The doctors put the fear of God in Cindy, so she followed their instructions. She took the time she needed and stayed as still and quiet as possible to give her back the time it needed to heal.

During her time recuperating, Cindy experienced a range of emotions. She says she was scared on many different levels. She wondered if she would ever skate again. She was also ashamed that she had lost her temper and hurt herself. When Cindy came to the realization that she would have to go home to the United States, she felt lost, alone and unsure of what the future held. The only thing she knew, deep in her heart, was that she had to do what the doctors told her to do if she hoped to be able to start over again.

Cindy was in a Catholic hospital for about four to six weeks before they allowed her to return to the US. They wanted to make sure Cindy's healing was progressing well enough for her to make an 18-hour flight back home, without causing more serious injury to her damaged nerves. Unfortunately, Cindy's mom was not able to visit her while she was in the hospital overseas. Cindy knew her mom was scared to death and didn't know exactly what had happened to her daughter. Cindy was well taken care of, though, by the nuns in the hospital.

Cindy recalls the nuns being stern but funny, and they made sure Cindy did what the doctor ordered. Cindy says the nuns kept her spirits high and gave her such inner strength, even if she was not the best patient, due to her pain.

The nuns brought meals into Cindy's room, and would tell her that she had to eat everything on her plate, so that she could heal and grow strong again. The only problem was that when Cindy cleaned her plate, the next plate had more food on it. Cindy started gaining weight, which they thought was great, because they informed her she was too skinny and needed to get some meat on her bones. Cindy thought the nuns were absolutely fantastic. They helped her both physically and mentally. Cindy realized they were taking the best possible care of her in a very compassionate and loving manner. They made Cindy strong. Of the nuns, Cindy says, "I owe them so very much, because they gave me so very much."

Once the doctors cleared Cindy for travel, Ralphie set up a Cindy McCoy farewell night at each of the stadiums: Sydney, Brisbane and Melbourne, where Cindy was able to say goodbye to her fans. She says the ovations all of the fans gave to her was incredible. She received all kinds of well wishes, beautiful flowers, candy and gifts. Cindy remembers some fans even arriving at the airport to send her off. Cindy felt as though she was leaving family.

Dennis, the President of the Cindy McCoy Fan Club in Brisbane, and the members of the club, were awesome to Cindy, and she would miss them all very much. They had welcomed Cindy into their hearts and homes. Even though Cindy told her fans she would return one day, she knew in her heart she would probably never get the chance to return to the wonderful home she had found Down Under.

Chapter Eleven

After returning to the United States, Cindy wrote letters to several of the fan club members and through the letters, she learned that Dennis had died of a bleeding ulcer. It was such sad news for her. The fans kept Cindy up to date on what was going on Down Under, but it made her sad because she wasn't there skating and enjoying their company. They told Cindy they were incorporating more Australians into the sport, but they preferred to watch the Americans skate. Unfortunately, attendance started to decline, because the fans wanted to see Americans, not Australians. Cindy felt as though the special Australian/American connection and bond was being lost.

The office in LA asked Cindy if she would consider going to Japan to skate once she was released from her doctors' care. Cindy told them her preference was to go back to Australia to skate. She could tell by their tone of voice that it would never happen. They were planning on closing down in Australia, which they never told Cindy directly, but she knew it intuitively. Soon after, Cindy stopped corresponding with her Australian fans because it hurt to know that she would never return to Australia, and she didn't have the heart to tell them. Cindy realized now it was a very bad decision on her part. She realizes she should have never done that to them. They were Cindy's true friends, and in the end, Cindy feels she let them down in a very poor fashion. Cindy believes they would have never done that to her. She feels a lot of regret for that decision and is now truly sorry.

Once Cindy received her release, she told the administration that she did not want to skate in Japan. Instead, Cindy was picked up for a series by the visiting team in Los Angeles. Toni Tagg was the captain and Dave Pound was the coach. They were two very powerful and strong skaters. This would be the first time Cindy would skate in a different uniform, against the local LA T/birds.

Toni broke her leg in the first game of the series, and Cindy remembers how upset she was; she had no faith in the young females on her team. Toni's replacement, Diane S., who was also a second year professional skater like Cindy and did the defending while Toni was out, was not one of Cindy's favorite people. Both she and Cindy had started out as amateurs, and they did not get along. Cindy thought she was a very spiteful person, and was out to show everyone that she was better, and badder than Cindy was. Obviously, there was tension on the squad before they even took to the track.

Cindy was a little nervous about being on the track skating once again after her injury. She had a lot of obvious concerns. She was afraid of hurting herself again. This was the first time she had to deal with her own personal fear on the track. However, once she warmed up and the whistle blew, all of that fear and concern left her. The sound of the crowd, the sound of the skates on the track, and the air in her face, made her feel at home. She was back where she belonged. And she was stronger and faster than ever.

When Cindy was out on the jam, she came up to the rear of the pack and was getting into scoring position. She thought it was going to be good. But then, Diane S., who was being a spiteful bitch, blocked Cindy and took her out. Cindy couldn't believe the woman would do that to her own teammate. Cindy was furious and Toni was screaming at both of them, threatening to take them out of the game. Cindy yelled back at Toni and said, "Keep that bitch away from me!"

The game continued, but the tension kept building between Diane S. and Cindy. Finally, Cindy made up her mind that she would score without Diane's help. And Cindy would do everything in her power to make sure the bitch did not take her out again. Cindy out-skated her, put a trip block on her and went about the business of scoring points. This was the strongest Cindy had ever been, and she never held back. Cindy went full-out and no one was going to stop her. Cindy could see the fans were going wild because the game was so powerful. Cindy could also hear the roar of the crowd. The louder they got, the faster she tried to go. And go she did!

After that series, Cindy gained a tremendous amount of confidence. She knew she could hold her own against the best players. Cindy knew she would never return to Australia, and she knew it was time for her to move on with my life. But Cindy wanted to go out at the top of her game.

If she was going to return to her birth home, and finish school like she had promised her mom, she wanted to do justice to the roller games she had grown to love. Even if her days as a professional skater were coming to end, Cindy was leaving the game on her own terms, in a blaze of glory.

Chapter Twelve

After completing her final series, Cindy talked with her mom, and she agreed that it was time for them to return to Colorado Springs, Colorado. The home situation with Tex was getting even worse. He had become very aggressive, and Cindy finally snapped and attacked him.

Cindy purchased an old '54 blue and white Ford for her own transportation to return to Colorado. She took the back seat out of it, and packed everything that would fit into the old Ford. Cindy affectionately named the vehicle, Leaping Leena. She and her mom were soon on their way back to Colorado via the old Route 66. Cindy prayed Leaping Leena would make it all the way.

When they arrived at Cindy's grandmother's home, Cindy started checking into the various schools and inquired about which one's would allow her to complete two years of school in one by taking extra classes to earn enough credits to graduate. The Air Academy High would allow Cindy to take extra classes, but they would require Cindy to live within the district. Cindy spoke with her Uncle Gene and Aunt Tammie to see if she could stay with them until she graduated. At the time, they lived in the Black Forest, which was in the school district.

Cindy had to get a part-time job, and do housework in exchange for room and board. The arrangements only lasted for about half of the year until Cindy got so angry with Tammie's jealousy and lying that she had to make other living arrangements.

Cindy talked with her homeroom teacher. She was having problems with her daughter, Gretchen, and was trying to keep her in school until she graduated. Cindy and her teacher made a deal. Cindy befriended Gretchen to keep her in school, and Cindy lived with them until graduation. As a result of her deal with her homeroom teacher, Cindy was able to keep her promise to her mom. She graduated one year later than if she had stayed in school rather than skating.

Cindy was offered a college scholarship, which she declined, because she wasn't sure what she was going to do with the rest of her life. Cindy participated in a summer course on the military base. She did data entry on the old punch card system. She received a Pride Achievement Award from the Air Force Academy as a result of her work on base. Cindy followed up the internship with working at the First National Bank of Colorado Springs. She started in the BAC department. Credit cards were just becoming popular and Cindy's job was to contact businesses about putting credit card machines into their place of operations. Cindy did this for some time until she transferred into the audit department.

The bank was involved with the yearly racecar hill climb up Pike's Peak and Cindy was cornered into helping out with the race. She worked as a pacer. As a result of the work, Cindy got involved in the Miss Colorado Springs program because they needed bodies. At first, Cindy really didn't want to get involved with it, since it was for scholarships, and she really didn't have any idea what was truly involved.

Mr. Beals, one of Cindy's bosses at the First National Bank, made a strong suggestion that Cindy participate in the pageant for the bank and for the city. Because Cindy believed they needed participants, she agreed to go forward with the competition. The lady running the pageant for the city was a good, long-time customer of the bank. She was such a nice lady, and Cindy enjoyed doing what she could to help her out.

Everything was going along fine until Cindy ran into one big issue—she needed to have some kind of talent! Cindy felt very short in this category, and she kept telling them she had no talent. They insisted, however, that she come up with something to do. Cindy kept telling them that the only thing she was good at was roller skating and horseback riding, but she couldn't do these things on the small stage where the contestants had to perform.

After a lot of discussions over this issue, Cindy agreed to do the number, "There is Nothing Like a Dame" from South Pacific. Cindy knew it would be a difficult sale, because she could not actually carry a tune. Instead, she made the number into a comic type of routine to hide the big fact she couldn't sing. During the routine, Cindy was to drop her pants (the whites), which she was fine with, but on the night of the competition, she couldn't get her pants to drop. The rope tie was in a knot, and she had a terrible time with it. No matter how hard she shook to get the pants to drop, they wouldn't go down. Cindy remembers saying, "Oh shit, they won't go down." She went into a clown-type mode and had the people in the audience cracking up because they thought her antics were all part of the skit. The audience applauded the performance, but Cindy was horrified. In the end, everything worked out fine. Cindy was a clown, but she just hadn't known it. Cindy was a finalist in the 1969 Miss Colorado Springs competition.

~ ~ ~ ~ ~

When she was 21 years old, Cindy's mother told Cindy that her sister had passed away. It was a tremendous and devastating loss for Cindy.

Cindy confronted her mom and told her that she was never really a mother to Corrine. Cindy says she was angry at her mother and lashed out. She said some mean and hateful things out of hurt, anger and lack of understanding. Her mother had left Cindy and her sister and had left more than once. Cindy said, "You dumped Corrine, remember? And you abandoned me twice, remember?" When her mom told Cindy that she had difficulty coping, Cindy thought she was being dramatic and shot back, "But you could cope with the sleazer you brought home because it suited you. It was always about you. What you wanted. What your pleasure was. Well, now you're free." Cindy says her mom seemed to take good care of Corrine when she was home, so she never understood why her parents could not continue to physically care for her sister and why they needed the extra help.

All Cindy ever wanted was a family: her mother, sister and dad. It was something she only had for a short period of time her life. It was something she was able to recreate to an extent when she went to Australia, but even that came to an abrupt end.

Chapter Thirteen

Cindy married her first husband, Stewart Mathews, in 1970. He graduated from the University of Northern Colorado. He also served in the armed forces with the 101st Airborne Division. He and Cindy had two children, Sean and Tiffany. They were married for 12½ years before they divorced. During her first marriage, Cindy worked at a bank then went to work for an accounting firm. She stayed home with her children for a while and did daycare out of her home, before getting into the restaurant business.

Cindy says her first husband became a different person from the one she married. Years later, Cindy found out that he was bipolar, and his consumption of alcohol made this medical issue much worse. Back in those days, Cindy had no idea what she was dealing with. Cindy left the marriage because she was afraid of his mood swings, and she felt her life was in danger, as well as that her children. Stewart passed away in 2010 in Phoenix, Arizona.

After the divorce from her first husband, Cindy continued to work in all aspects of the restaurant business. She was a bookkeeper, waitress, cook, assistant manager and promotions specialist. She also worked as a general manager of a video rental store. Cindy eventually put herself through Metropolitan State College, where she earned her BS degree.

Cindy lost her mom to lung cancer in 1988. Cindy and her paternal aunt, (Ada) Mildred Proctor, had taken care of her until she passed away. Cindy says, "Cancer is an ugly way to die. I loved my mom and it really broke my heart to watch her die of lung cancer."

In 1999, Cindy married her current husband, Terrance G. O'Neill. He was born in Albany, NY and spent 22 years in the navy. He earned his BS Degree from National University of San Diego in

1988. He served in the Vietnam Era and was involved in the fall of Saigon in April 1975 and the last naval battle, Operation Praying Mantis, in April 1988. He was detained in Cambodia for almost two years on a mission that never happened. Terry was the highest decorated enlisted man on board the USS Bagley.

Cindy and Terry met when she was an assistant manager of a convenience store and she was tasked with training him to be a manager. Cindy said she was told to be extremely hard on him to ensure he would develop into a strong store manager. She followed orders and made it her mission to make Terry's job difficult.

When she was reassigned to another store to cover for a manager, who was injured, Terry was left on his own and did turn into a strong store manager. Cindy obtained an injury, and had to have surgery on her rib. She would walk down to Terry's store to talk with him and keep the promotions going for the store.

Once she was released from her medical leave, the store she'd been managing closed, so she had no place to return to work. Terry needed a strong assistant manager, so he hired Cindy to fill the position.

Terry's marriage had been on the rocks, so he obtained a divorce and married Cindy. Today, they have three beautiful grandchildren: Dylan, Faith, and Alivia. Cindy also has a stepson, Raymond.

In 2006, Cindy and Terry were involved in a serious car accident, in which they both sustained multiple injuries. Terry underwent rotator cuff surgery, as well as having both of his hands operated on. He also had hip surgery to repair Librium tears and has had to undergo multiple spine injections to relieve the pain in his lower back.

Cindy was hospitalized following the accident because she had no feeling in her arms and legs and was dizzy and nauseous. She had injuries to her neck, rotator cuff, lower back, hip and knees. If the paramedics had not stabilized her neck, Cindy could have been paralyzed from the neck down as a result of the neck injuries she sustained.

Cindy underwent neck surgery, in which they fussed the 3rd, 4th, 5th and 6th vertebra. She also had surgery on her rotator cuff and, like Terry, has had a series of epidural injections in the neck and back for pain as well as steroid injections into the hips and knees.

Both Cindy and Terry have had to spend hundreds of hours in physical and occupational therapy to overcome and adapt to their physical limitations as a result of the accident. Cindy says that the accident and neck surgery has caused bone spurs to grow above her 3rd vertebra that will eventually require another operation. Because the surgeons will have to go in from the back of the neck to saw off the spurs, Cindy is putting off the procedure until she can no longer control the pain.

During her skating days, Cindy sustained nerve damage, which caused her to lose feeling in her legs. The auto accident added to this condition, and she has lost more feeling in her legs. Cindy has always been tough and she never let physical limitations stop her from fulfilling her dreams. She deals with her current condition one day at a time. The sense of determination that made Cindy a superstar athlete will most certainly get her through any hardships she might face in the future. With strength, courage and resolve, she will continue to rehabilitate herself.

~ ~ ~ ~ ~

In the 21st century, roller derby has undergone resurgence in popularity. Today, there are more than 1,200 amateur leagues throughout the world and the sport is being considered for the 2020 Olympics.

Thanks to the trailblazers like Cindy McCoy and the other women, who skated in the tough sport, long before the era of women's liberation, roller derby in the 21st century is now a female-dominated sport. Popular films, such as *Whip It*, directed by Drew Barrymore and starring Ellen Page, have also made the sport more accessible to the younger generations and have helped to grow a new fan base for the sport's revival.

In May 2010, Cindy had the honor to be named an Honorary Member of the Denver Roller Dolls. Cindy was presented an award in front of an audience of seven thousand roller derby fans, many of them young people, who are the new generation of enthusiasts. Cindy was given a standing ovation. Cindy was lauded as being an inspiration to all roller derby hopefuls during the past four decades and appreciation was expressed for her unfailing contribution to the sport. Cindy says it was truly heart-warming to receive the award and to be recognized as one of the pioneers of the sport of roller games.

The event brought back so many memories for Cindy and for the older fans, who remember the sport and how it was in its heyday. Cindy stopped and took notice of how much the games meant to all of the fans. It had been 45 years since she had experienced that type of applause when she was a teen Rookie Roller Queen.

Photo Gallery

ALIVA BOLT, CINDY'S GRAND DAUGHTER; TERRY O'NEILL, CINDY'S HUSBAND; MILDRED PROCTOR, CINDY'S AUNT; FAITH ALEXIS BOLT, CINDY'S GRANDDAUGHTER; CINDY AND DYLAN BOLT, CINDY'S GRANDSON

CINDY'S GRANDCHILDREN at play

CINDY and her AUNT MILDRED PROCTOR

113

CINDY and SADIE

CINDY and TERRY O'NEILL

WEDDING PHOTO

CINDY'S DAUGHTER, TIFFANY BOLT with
AUNT MILDRED

CINDY and her son, SEAN JASON
MATHEWS

Cindy McCoyWebsite

Visit the Cindy McCoy website for:

Additional Information and Updates

Social Networking/Connect with Fans

Historic Photos and Videos

Cindy McCoy's Emporium

(Apparel/Accessories /Memorabilia/Gifts)

www.rollerderbylegend.com

Printed in Great Britain
by Amazon.co.uk, Ltd.,
Marston Gate.